50 THINGS YOU DIDN'T KNOW ABOUT

ANCIENT GREECE

Written and Illustrated
by Sean O'Neill

RED CHAIR PRESS
Egremont, Massachusetts

50 Things You Didn't Know About is produced and published by Red Chair Press:
Red Chair Press LLC PO Box 333 South Egremont, MA 01258

LC record available at https://lccn.loc.gov/2019931709

First softcover edition ISBN: 978-1-63440-799-1

Printed in the United States of America

0822 2P CGS20

TABLE of CONTENTS

Chapter 1:
GOVERNMENT & WARFARE 4

Chapter 2:
GODS & MYTHOLOGY 10

Chapter 3:
DAILY LIFE 16

Chapter 4:
TECHNOLOGY & PHILOSOPHY 22

Chapter 5:
THE OLYMPIC GAMES 26

Glossary 30

Explore More 31

Index/About the Author 32

CHAPTER 1

GOVERNMENT & WARFARE

Ancient Greece may bring to mind legendary gods and heroes battling mythical monsters, but it was actually a thriving and complex society. Ancient Greece refers to various civilizations that inhabited the Greek peninsula and islands from 2000 B.C.E to 30 B.C.E. The height of Greek culture was in the fifth century B.C.E. Although the Greeks frequently warred with both their neighbors and each other, they are responsible for developing sophisticated systems of government and social order, many of which are still in use today.

1 The civilization of Ancient Greece includes several different periods, including Minoan, Mycenaean, Classical, and Hellenistic.

2 Ancient Greece was made up of as many as 2,000 city-states. The most powerful were Athens and Sparta.

3 The city of Athens is named after the goddess Athena.

4 Athenian citizens had to do jury duty. 6,000 citizens had to serve each year, and a single jury could have as many as 500 jurors!

5 The world's first **democracy** was formed in ancient Athens. Citizens could participate in a large meeting called the Assembly.

6 The word democracy means "Power of the People."

7 In ancient Greece, the word "idiot" meant anyone who didn't participate in politics.

8 Citizens would sometimes vote using dried beans. This is where we get the expression, "spill the beans," which means to tell the truth or reveal a secret.

9 When citizens wanted to banish a politician, they voted by writing his name on a piece of pottery called an *ostrakon*. This is where we get the word **ostracize**, which means exclude, or send away.

10 The most famous Greek leader of all time, Alexander the Great, was actually from Macedonia. Alexander was the first leader to put his face on coins.

11 After 800 B.C.E., the city of Sparta had no walls because the Spartan king considered his soldiers strong enough to defend the city.

12 An Athenian warship called a *trireme* was powered by 170 oarsmen.

13 Greek soldiers had to be strong. They wore 70 pounds (32 kg) of bronze armor!

14 Spartan men could be called to military service from the age of 20 until they turned 60. Although, not many Spartan soldiers lived that long!

CHAPTER 2

GODS & MYTHOLOGY

Ancient Greece, like Egypt before it, was a ***polytheistic*** society, and the Greeks had many gods and goddesses that were believed to live atop Mount Olympus. From there the gods observed, and often interfered with, the lives of humans. Although the stories of the gods, titans, and heroes of mythology may be familiar, some of the more unusual beliefs and traditions of the Greeks may surprise you.

15 Athena is the daughter of Zeus. She was believed to have emerged from Zeus's head after it was cut open by the blacksmith god Hephaistos.

16 It was believed that Athena brought the olive tree to Athens.

17 Prometheus, who was believed to have given humans fire, was punished by the gods by having his liver eaten by eagles. This was because Greeks believed the liver, rather than the heart, was thought to be the center of human emotions.

18 According to legend, the Greek army snuck into the walls of Troy by hiding inside a huge wooden horse. When the city of Troy was discovered in 1870, they didn't find the remains of the horse, but today there is a model of the Trojan Horse at the site.

19 The word "music" comes from the Muses, goddesses of the arts in Greek mythology.

20 The tradition of putting candles on a birthday cake started in ancient Greece when people brought cakes topped with lit candles to the temple of Artemis, goddess of the hunt. The candles were lit to make them glow like the moon, a symbol associated with Artemis.

21 The Greek city of Delphi was believed to be the center of the world. There was a huge stone placed there called the *omphalos*, or belly-button of the world.

22 After death it was believed that you journeyed across the river Styx to the underworld of Hades. As if that wasn't bad enough, you also had to pay one coin for a ticket to ride the ferry across!

23 At a Greek funeral the body was laid out with its feet facing the door to make sure the spirit would leave.

24 Greeks consulted an oracle, or priest, to get a message from the gods. People traveled from all over Greece to see the oracle at Delphi.

CHAPTER 3

DAILY LIFE

Daily life in Ancient Greece may not have been as exciting as the labors of Heracles or the journeys of Jason and the Argonauts, but citizens of cities like Athens and Sparta led rich and complex lives. Some of these lesser known details about Greek life will probably surprise you, but may also give you a clearer picture of what life was like for the many citizens of Ancient Greece.

25 In ancient Greece, throwing an apple at somebody was a declaration of love. Sometimes it was even used as a marriage proposal.

26 To color their clothing, Greeks used dyes made from sea snails and insect larva.

27 The tradition of walking the Red Carpet dates back to ancient Greece. The play *Agamemnon* mentions a "Crimson Path," a symbol of stature and luxury fit only for the gods.

28 A popular game was called "knucklebones" and was played with ankle joints of small goats and sheep.

29 Wine was the most popular drink in ancient Greece and it was enjoyed with all meals, including breakfast!

30 Spartans made a drink by mixing salt, vinegar, and blood. Yuck!

31 The Greeks loved plays, and many dramas by Greek playwrights such as Aeschylus are still performed today. They were so popular that many Greek theaters held up to 14,000 people.

32 A Greek instrument called a lyre used a tortoise shell for amplification.

33 Music and dance were very important parts of Greek culture. Songs were sung at births, weddings, and funerals. Popular Greek dances included "The Itch," "The Snort," and "Setting the World on Fire."

34 Most professions were closed to female citizens, but women were allowed to do a few jobs, including tending horses, playing music, and selling perfume and clothing.

35 Greek schoolchildren wrote by scratching on wooden tablets covered with wax. They used a sharpened stick made from bone or metal. It even had a blunt end for smoothing out mistakes—the original eraser!

36 Girls were married at age 14 or 15. On the day before the wedding she burned her dolls and toys.

37 Greek sheepdogs on farms wore spiked collars, called *melium*, to protect their necks from wolf bites as they defended flocks of sheep.

CHAPTER 4

TECHNOLOGY & PHILOSOPHY

In addition to developing the first democratic system of government, ancient Greeks made many advances in science and technology. Famous Greek philosophers like Socrates, Plato and Aristotle considered the meaning of existence and humans' place in the universe. Their discoveries laid the groundwork for societies throughout history all the way up to our own.

38 A Greek physician named Hippocrates was the creator of the Hippocratic Oath, which is still taken by doctors today.

39 Greek philosopher Aristotle was a teacher for the future **emperor** Alexander the Great.

40 A counting tool called an *abacus* was one of the world's first calculators. It used beads strung on a wire to make calculations.

41 Some philosophers believed beans contained the **reincarnated** souls of the dead and shouldn't be eaten.

42 The Parthenon sits at the top of the Acropolis in Athens and was originally a temple to the goddess Athena. The Acropolis was destroyed in the Persian wars of the 5th century B.C.E. It was rebuilt 30 years later and has survived for over 2000 years.

43 Ancient Greeks invented the first vending machine! This ancient machine was in a temple and sold holy water. When the proper coin was placed into the slot, the mouth at the bottom would open and holy water would pour out and the customer could fill their jar.

44 The Queen of Knossos on the island of Crete had the world's first flushing toilet!

45 Greek mathematician Euclid invented geometry, so blame him if you're having trouble in math class!

CHAPTER 5

THE OLYMPIC GAMES

The Olympic Games started in Ancient Greece and the tradition continues today. The games were held every four years at the temple of Zeus in Olympia, and were one of the most popular events in Greek society. Athletic competition was so important to the Greeks that they would often take a break from their many wars and battles in order to peacefully compete in the games.

46 The first Olympic games were held in 776 B.C.E. The modern Olympics began in 1896, with the first games being held in Athens, of course.

47 The ancient Olympics included the events boxing, discus, javelin, and running, all of which are still Olympic events. The most popular sport was wrestling.

48 Winners at the Olympics didn't win medals, or money, or prizes. They received a crown of olive leaves called a laurel. And the honor and respect of their fellow citizens, of course.

49 There wasn't television in ancient Greece. But even if there had been, the Olympics wouldn't be shown because the athletes competed naked!

50 The modern marathon distance of 26.2 miles is based on a legend of an ancient Greek messenger that ran from the city of Marathon to Athens, a distance of about 40 kilometers, or 25 miles, to bring news of a military victory over the Persians. The legend states that the exhausted messenger dropped dead after giving the news.

WE WON!!
YEAH!
VICTORY!
HOORAY!
PRAISE ZEUS!
YAY!!
UH... GUYS..?
MARATHON 25 MILES
GREEKS WIN!

Glossary

democracy: a form of government where people have the power to chose the leaders

emperor: the (male) ruler of an Empire

ostracize: to exclude or ignore someone

polytheistic: believing that there are many gods

reincarnate: to give another life and/or body to a spirit

Explore Greece More

Books

Pearson, Anne. *Ancient Greece* (DK Eyewitness Books). DK Childrens' Publishing, 2014.

Napoli, Donna Jo. *Treasury of Greek Mythology: Classic Stories of Gods, Goddesses, Heroes & Monsters*. National Geographic Kids, 2011.

Newman, Sandra. *Ancient Greece* (True Books). Scholastic, 2010.

Osborne, Mary Pope and **Boyce, Natalie Pope**. *Ancient Greece and the Olympics* (Magic Tree House). Random House for Young Readers, 2004.

On the Web

DK find out!

https://www.dkfindout.com/us/history/ancient-greece/

Index

Acropolis 24
Alexander the Great 7, 23
Artemis. 14
Athena 5, 11, 24
Crete. 25
Delphi. 14, 15
Euclid 25
Hades 15
Heracles 16
Hippocrates 23
Mount Olympus. 10
Prometheus. 12
Sparta. 5, 8, 16
Troy 13
Zeus 11, 26

About the Author/Illustrator

Sean O'Neill is an illustrator and writer living in Chicago. He is the creator of the *Rocket Robinson* series of graphic novels. Sean loves history, trivia, and drawing cartoons, so this project is pretty much a dream assignment. And it comes with Olympic athletes!